D1135236

Older

but not wiser

This book is dedicated to anyone old enough for
it to have sunk in that ageing is a one-way trip

First published in the United Kingdom in 2014 by
Portico
43 Great Ormond Street
London
WC1N 3HZ

An imprint of Pavilion Books Company Ltd

ISBN 978 1 90939 638 8

A CIP catalogue record for this book is available from the British Library.

10 9 8 7

Design: Suzanne Perkins/grafica
Colour reproduction by Dot Gradations Ltd, UK
Printed and bound by Toppan Leefung Printing Ltd, China
This book can be ordered direct from the publisher at www.pavilionbooks.com

THE WIT AND
Cath Tate
WISDOM OF

Older

but not wiser

PORTICO

Getting older starts
at a very young age.

Growing older is not the
same as growing up.

Women
don't grow older, they just discover themselves.

Age doesn't matter, unless you're a cheese.

The secret of staying young
is to live honestly, eat slowly
and lie about your age.

The more candles
on your cake,
the hotter you are.

It's quite important to have *several* 30th birthdays in one lifetime.

Never trust anyone over 30.

The ten best years
of a woman's life are
between 39 and 59.

"I've never been so old as I am today."

The hardest years are those between 6 and 60.

Age and treachery
will triumph over
youth and skill.

" To get back my youth
I would do anything
in the world,

except exercise,
get up early or be
respectable."

Youth would be ideal
if it came a little later in life.

The secret of eternal
youth is to make a
complete twit of yourself.

"At my age I can say exactly what I like."

"A telegram from the queen? Do I know her?"

"Yes, mother, I am old enough to remember landlines."

"I'm getting older every year, but not *quite* so much as my friends."

Growing old is compulsory.
Growing up is optional.

" I'm old enough now
to drink myself into an
early grave."

"My level of maturity
depends on
whom I am with."

Act the age you feel.

It's hard being young, but even harder staying there.

It's not how old you grow,
but how you grow old.

Old enough
to know better.

Young enough
to do it anyway.

"No, I don't want double glazing. Would you like to hear about my operation?"

"As the years go by,
I keep on losing weight
but it keeps on finding me."

The trouble with having
bags under your eyes…

…is finding the shoes
to match.

Never let middle age
creep up on you.

Inside every middle-aged woman is a 14-year-old trying to get out.

You're only
middle-aged once.

Middle age is when your
broad mind and narrow
waist change places.

Middle age had not dimmed their passion.

"We're not
over the hill, we're
only halfway up it."

"We're not old, we're retro."

"At my age,
it helps to slip into
something comfortable,
like denial."

"Grow old with me.
The best is yet to come."

"Let us grow old together,
you and I...

...you first."

"I'm going to retire
and live off my savings.

What I'll do on the second
day I'm not sure."

"When I retire I shall spend all my time pestering my friends to sign petitions."

Retirement is
something for the young.
Once you're old
you never have the time.

Look out!
The HRT gang has hit town!

Old age ain't no place for sissies.

Make hay, before you're put out to grass.

"I don't hear as well as I did, but I never used to listen anyway."

As you get older,
you find your eyes, ears and
teeth become detachable.

"I'm not old. I'm just
suffering from
Youth Deficiency Syndrome."

"If I'd known
I was going to live this long,
I'd have taken better
care of myself."

If you give up smoking,
drinking and sex,
you don't live longer,
it just feels like it.

The only way to have a
long and happy life…

...is to get old.

"If I had my life over again, I'd make the same mistakes...

...only sooner!"

Whatever your age –
never apologise,
never explain.

Don't worry. You'll be even
older tomorrow.

Cath Tate has lived and worked in London for more years than she cares to mention. She currently runs a greeting card company, Cath Tate Cards, with her daughter Rosie: the bulk of the photos and captions in this book started life as greetings cards.

The photos have been collected over the years by Cath and her friends in junk shops and vintage fairs. They are all genuine and show people in all their glory, on the beach, on a day out, posing stiffly for the photographer, drinking with friends, smiling or scowling at the camera.

The photographs were all taken sometime between 1880 and 1960. Times change but people, their friendships, their little joys and stupid mistakes, remain the same. Some things have changed though, and Cath Tate has used modern technical wizardry to tease some colour into the cheeks of those whose cheeks lost their colour some time ago.

The quotes that go with the photos come from random corners of life and usually reflect some current concern that is bugging her.

If you want to see all the current greetings cards and other ephemera available from Cath Tate Cards see www.cathtatecards.com

Cath Tate

Many thanks to all those helped me put this book together, including Discordia, who have fed me with wonderful photos and ideas over the years, and Suzanne Perkins, who has made sure everything looks OK, and also has a good line in jokes.

Picture credits

Photos from the collection of Cath Tate apart from the following:
Discordia/Simon: Pages 6–7, 18–19, 40–41, 48–49, 60–61, 66–67, 84–85
Discordia/Kulturrecycling: Pages 102–103
Keith Allen: Pages 34–35, 88–89
Mary Bristow-Jones: Pages 90–91